CARDS OF
CHARACTER
>>→ FOR ←≪
BRAVE
BOYS

CARDS OF CHARACTER

FOR

BRAVE BOYS

SHAREABLE
DEVOTIONS &
ENCOURAGEMENT

BARBOUR **kidz**
A Division of Barbour Publishing

Scripture quotations marked NIV are taken from the HOLY BIBLE, NEW INTERNATIONAL VERSION®. NIV®. Copyright © 1973, 1978, 1984, 2011 by Biblica, Inc.™ Used by permission. All rights reserved worldwide.

Scripture quotations marked NLT are taken from the *Holy Bible*. New Living Translation copyright© 1996, 2004, 2015 by Tyndale House Foundation. Used by permission of Tyndale House Publishers, Inc. Carol Stream, Illinois 60188. All rights reserved.

Scripture quotations marked ESV are from The Holy Bible, English Standard Version®, copyright © 2001 by Crossway Bibles, a publishing ministry of Good News Publishers. Used by permission. All rights reserved.

Scripture quotations marked NLV are taken from the New Life Version copyright © 1969 and 2003 by Barbour Publishing, Inc. All rights reserved.

Published by Barbour Publishing Inc., 1810 Barbour Drive, Uhrichsville, Ohio 44683, www.barbourbooks.com

Our mission is to inspire the world with the life-changing message of the Bible.

Printed in China.

000550 0121 HA

BRAVE BOYS
➤→ HAVE CHARACTER! ←←

You'll discover just who God made you to be with these tear-out, shareable Cards of Character, featuring important messages that brave boys need to hear.

Flip each page to discover an important, challenging life message that will encourage your heart and the hearts of other brave boys just like you. Once you've read through each devotion and wisdom-filled take-away, tear out the cards and hang them up as wonderful reminders of the brave boy God created you to be. . .or share them with other brave boys like you!

P.S. With your parents' permission, check out forbraveboys.com where you'll discover positive, faith-building activities and resources!

A PLAN FOR VICTORY!

What are you good at? Skateboarding, gaming, Ping-Pong?

We all have skills. Sometimes we win a trophy, plaque, or ribbon for being the best at what we do. The trophies get displayed, pictures are taken, and memories are made.

A lot of hard work goes into achieving anything really special. Sometimes this means we get up early, practice more, and work up a sweat.

God wants us to achieve one thing more than others. What He wants may mean we get up early, practice hard, and use some energy.

When you play basketball you can't win a game by sitting on the bench. When you're in a scholar's bowl you'll fail if you never study. When you live for God you can't grow by refusing to follow the rules.

There are those around us who don't want us to succeed. They want us to make poor choices. They want us to lose interest in what God wants.

The only way we can win is to believe that God's plan for our lives can be trusted, that His truth should be followed, and that we're most like Him when we obey.

For every child of God defeats this evil world, and we achieve this victory through our faith.
1 JOHN 5:4 NLT

GOD wants you to win. In fact, He has a plan for your victory. Follow Him and see what He has in store for you!

(Pass It On! Share this encouraging message with another brave boy just like you!)

DON'T BRING ME DOWN!

⋙————————————➤

Imagine standing on a chair while a friend stands in front of you on the floor. When someone says "Go," you attempt to pull your friend up onto the chair, while your friend tries just as hard to pull you down to the floor. Who do you think will win?

Have you ever noticed how our personalities can change when we are around certain people? How you act around your family is probably different from how you act around your friends. We all want to fit in, to be like our friends. And our first response is to mimic our friends' actions, whether good or bad. When a friend makes bad choices, we're tugged toward bad choices too. The Bible tells us to choose our friends wisely, because bad friends can cause us to do things we know are wrong. Just like the chair exercise, it's easier for a bad friend to pull us down and get us to follow him than it is to pull a bad friend up to follow after good.

If you find yourself being pulled down, hang in there! Ask God for help, and He will draw you close to Himself.

The righteous choose their friends carefully, but the way of the wicked leads them astray.
PROVERBS 12:26 NIV

BE A GOOD FRIEND
WHO ALWAYS LIFTS
OTHERS UP!

(Pass It On! Share this encouraging message
with another brave boy just like you!)

WHO WE HANG OUT WITH

Friends are pretty wonderful. They listen to you, enjoy the same stuff, and are fun to hang out with.

God has always wanted us to be friendly to everyone. He invented love, so it just makes sense that we care about other people, but that doesn't mean all friends are created equal.

Some people want us to do things we know make God sad. Some think it's okay for you to follow God, but they don't want to. Other friends want to know God too.

We should hang out the most with others who love God. We want to be around those friends who want to grow closer to God and want us to grow with them.

God's Word says we should find friends who build us up in our faith. Our best friends should be the ones who help us want to be changed by God's gifts, and when we *do* make mistakes, these friends will encourage us to make things right as soon as possible.

Maybe you could be that kind of friend for someone today.

I am a friend to anyone who fears you—
anyone who obeys your commandments.
PSALM 119:63 NLT

MAKE FRIENDS WITH OTHER BRAVE BOYS WHO LOVE GOD MOST OF ALL. AND WORK HARD TO BE THAT KIND OF FRIEND TO OTHERS TOO!

(Pass It On! Share this encouraging message
with another brave boy just like you!)

ULTIMATE FORGIVENESS

Keeping score. Holding a grudge. Do you know someone who keeps track of wrongs done to him? Every time someone hurts him, bad-mouths him, double-crosses him, it gets tallied up in his mind and held close to his heart. Maybe you find it hard to let go of offenses against you.

Can you imagine if God kept a record of wrongs done to Him? Sins that we commit against God are wrong. The truth is, there wouldn't be enough books in the world to hold the number of wrongs done to God. But there's good news! Through salvation, we have ultimate forgiveness in Christ. Forgiveness is the key to tearing up that book of wrongs that we hold so closely in our lives too. If God can forgive *all* the sins committed against Him, we can forgive the ones committed against us. It's not always easy. Some wrongs may take a lifetime to forgive. But we can ask God, the example of forgiveness, to help us forgive.

If you, LORD, kept a record of sins, Lord,
who could stand? But with you there is forgiveness,
so that we can, with reverence, serve you.
PSALM 130:3–4 NIV

GOD wants you to let go and forgive anyone who has hurt you. Give Him all your pain and anger and ask Him to fill you with His love and peace instead.

WHAT'S LEFT TO WORRY ABOUT?

Sometimes the latest news can be frightening. Lots of bad things can happen. It has always been that way, at least since the first sin by Adam and Eve. People make bad choices. Those decisions cause hurt, anger, and disappointment. For many people those choices cause fear.

We should always be smart. This might mean that we stay away from things we know could be harmful, but the fear we feel is a waste of emotion and will never change the outcome.

Our fears could be about something we don't understand, about a location, or about a person. God never wants us to be afraid. If we really believe He is in control, then what's left to worry about?

God is always with us. God's got this.

Be strong. Be courageous. Be brave. Be bold. Be fearless. Be assured that the God who created you is able to care for you better than anyone who has ever lived.

"This is my command—be strong and courageous!
Do not be afraid or discouraged. For the LORD
your God is with you wherever you go."
JOSHUA 1:9 NLT

WHEN YOU'RE AFRAID, REMEMBER THAT GOD HAS PROMISED TO TAKE CARE OF EVERYTHING. HE'S GOT IT ALL UNDER CONTROL!

(Pass It On! Share this encouraging message
with another brave boy just like you!)

PET SIN

Everybody has one: a pet sin. You know, it's the sin you hang on to. You keep coming back to it like a favorite T-shirt. When life gets tough or things don't go as planned, it bubbles up from deep within and rears its ugly head. For some, it's pride, envy, worry, fear, rebellion, self-centeredness, disobedience, anger. . .you fill in the blank.

The Bible says "sin is crouching at your door; it desires to have you, but you must rule over it." Sin is always there, like a lion waiting to pounce. It wants to eat you alive. But with God's help, we are stronger than our sin, not the other way around.

If you are struggling with sin today, seek God in prayer. And ask for help from family and leaders in your church. You have the power to stand up against sin. . .and win!

"If you do what is right, will you not be accepted? But if you do not do what is right, sin is crouching at your door; it desires to have you, but you must rule over it."
GENESIS 4:7 NIV

Avoid the temptation to make excuses for your behavior. Instead, ask God to take control of your life and then ask Him for forgiveness when you need to.

WORK IS GOD'S IDEA

❯❯❯————————————————————❯

"Five more minutes, Mom!" "Do I have to clean my room *today*?" "I hate taking the trash out!"

Have you ever said any of these things? Maybe you said something similar today.

God wants us to spend time with Him every day, but He also knows that when we don't have something good to do, we can be tempted to do the wrong thing. Work is God's idea. It teaches responsibility, an attitude of service, and helps us discover purpose.

You don't have to have a job to work. You can serve others, help your family, or work to learn new skills. Doing nothing makes it much easier to continue doing nothing.

When you can't see anything good in the work you accomplish, you can begin to think that nothing good exists. You might think that there is no purpose, no promise, and no possibility of enjoying life.

That's why God wants us to do everything for Him. If we work for Him, then *everything* we do is meaningful.

A lazy person's way is blocked with briers,
but the path of the upright is an open highway.
PROVERBS 15:19 NLT

Ask GoD to help you learn the importance of work and to help you understand your purpose. Then Be willing to jump in and Do the work He's called you to!

(Pass It On! Share this encouraging message with another brave boy just like you!)

REASONS TO APPRECIATE OTHERS

Jesus wants us to love people. This includes those who take care of us, our friends, and those we've just met.

We show love by appreciating the good things others do for us. This can seem hard because it means we'll have to think about and name the good things that others do—out loud. It's easier with a parent who sacrifices to help us, but harder with a brother or sister who gets on our nerves. It might be easy with a pastor who is kind and helpful, but harder with a friend or neighbor whose great skill seems to be annoying people.

When you show appreciation, you're saying that the person you're talking to plays an important role in your life. They have value even when they are a little frustrating. That can be hard to admit, but it shows love and can be a way for God to improve your friendships.

"A new command I give you: Love one another.
As I have loved you, so you must love one another.
By this everyone will know that you are my
disciples, if you love one another."
JOHN 13:34–35 NIV

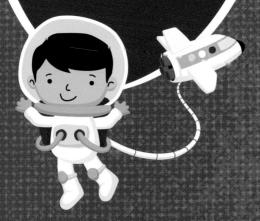

FOLLOW JESUS' EXAMPLE!
ASK HIM TO HELP YOU
SHOW LOVE AND
APPRECIATION
TO OTHERS.

(Pass It On! Share this encouraging message
with another brave boy just like you!)

AN HONORABLE DEMONSTRATION

⟫⟫⟫—————————————→

It's hard to believe that someone respects you when they do things they know you don't like. Respect means valuing other people by considering their needs as important as your own.

When the Bible gives us the "Golden Rule," we're reminded of something important to God. We show respect by honoring the interests, needs, and concerns of people who'll be happy to know you value them enough to be kind.

When we show respect to others, we often begin to receive respect in return. Showing honor to others doesn't mean you repay respect only when they're respectful. Sometimes you'll need to be the first to show honor. It doesn't even mean that you have to agree with their choices. It just means that you help them see that God can change the way Christians respond.

God treats us the way He wants to be treated too. He loved, showed faithfulness, and invited friendship first.

It's easier to respect others when we respect God first.

"Do to others whatever you would like them to do to you. This is the essence of all that is taught in the law and the prophets."
MATTHEW 7:12 NLT

GOD WANTS YOU TO SHOW HONOR TO OTHERS—WHETHER THEY'RE OLDER, YOUNGER, STRONGER, WEAKER, EASY TO LOVE, OR HARD TO LIKE!

(Pass It On! Share this encouraging message with another brave boy just like you!)

WHEN YOU DON'T FEEL LIKE IT

You don't have to plan on sinning to do the wrong thing. Sin is easy to find, looks like a lot of fun, and never reminds you of the consequences.

Sin is an easier choice than obedience. Maybe that's because our feelings love sin. People excuse their sin by saying it felt right or that they were having so much fun they couldn't help themselves.

Avoiding sin is a decision you should make before you get into a situation where it *feels* like you have no choice but to sin. If you know God doesn't want you to lie, then you need to decide that truth is what will come out of your mouth.

Jesus said that keeping His commandments (obedience) is the best way to show that we love Him. He didn't say, "If you love me, apologize daily."

We'll get it wrong. We'll sin. We'll wonder why we didn't obey. This is why God made sure we'd always be forgiven through Jesus' death on the cross.

Instead of seeking God's forgiveness as our regular reaction, we should avoid sin by obeying God—even when we don't *feel* like it.

[Jesus said], "If you love me, keep my commands."
JOHN 14:15 NIV

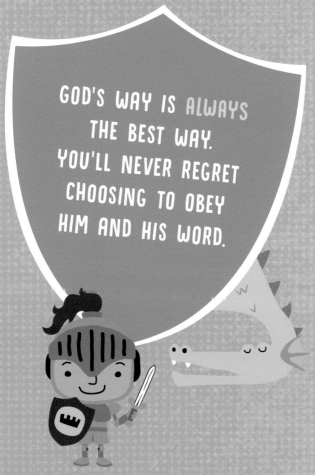

GOD'S WAY IS ALWAYS THE BEST WAY. YOU'LL NEVER REGRET CHOOSING TO OBEY HIM AND HIS WORD.

(Pass It On! Share this encouraging message with another brave boy just like you!)

NO ACTING REQUIRED

Sometimes being on our best behavior is like acting on stage. We say and do one thing, but it's not really who we are or what we believe. That's why just trying to behave never works very long. It's much easier to be yourself than to act like someone different.

Telling the truth, being nice to friends, and showing kindness are things your family would be proud to see in you. If you think you might be acting when you behave this way, be patient. God may have big plans for you.

The fruit of the Spirit is proof that God is working in your life. When you obey what God asks, you will be more loving, joyful, peaceful, patient, kind, good, faithful, gentle, and self-controlled. No acting required.

God wants you to do the right thing, but by growing as a Christian those "right things" become much easier because when you obey God you get closer to the plans He's always had for you.

The fruit of the Spirit is love, joy,
peace, forbearance, kindness, goodness,
faithfulness, gentleness and self-control.
GALATIANS 5:22–23 NIV

Stop for a minute and think about the value in obeying God's word. Be patient enough to notice His plans come together in your life, as you become the brave boy He created you to be!

(Pass It On! Share this encouraging message with another brave boy just like you!)

SETTING HIS EXAMPLE

⟫━━━━━━━━━━━━━━━➤

When you don't love someone, it's difficult to stand up for them when they're in trouble. When you don't love, it's easy to be afraid. When you have no love for other people, you can't stand strong because you never see anything worth fighting for.

God created us to be guardians, ambassadors, soldiers, and guys who care about other people.

He wants us to set His example for others to see. We never need to apologize for doing the right thing. We stand up for His truth and for those who need encouragement. He's given us a big job with big responsibilities, opportunities, and just the right amount of adventure.

We stand for something more important than sports and hobbies. We are strong in sharing a message that changes lives. We are courageous because everyone needs to know Jesus. We love because He loved us first.

The message we share can change lives. Refusing to speak up when someone really needs to hear what we have to say doesn't help them see the love we're supposed to share. Be courageous. Speak up.

Be on guard. Stand firm in the faith. Be courageous.
Be strong. And do everything with love.
1 Corinthians 16:13–14 NLT

SPEAK UP!
GOD'S MESSAGE IS
ALWAYS WORTH
SHARING!

(Pass It On! Share this encouraging message
with another brave boy just like you!)

WITHIN THE FENCE

When the Bible tells us to "follow God's example," it means He leads and models how we should live. When He says we're "dearly loved children," we know He accepts us. When we "walk in love," we choose to follow God's greatest commandment. When we see what Jesus did to show His love for us, we understand how important love is to God.

God created everything with a purpose. That includes you. When you "walk in love," you're living within the boundary of His commands. Like a spiritual fence, God's commands give plenty of freedom as long as you stay within the border.

When a dog leaves the protection of a fenced yard it can get into trouble, get hurt, or get lost. There are many more good things inside the fence than outside.

Spiritual fences aren't designed to make you miss what you shouldn't do, but to give you the space to do something special using the safety of God's protection—within the fence.

Follow God's example, therefore, as dearly loved children and walk in the way of love, just as Christ loved us and gave himself up for us as a fragrant offering and sacrifice to God.
EPHESIANS 5:1–2 NIV

THERE IS JOY IN FOLLOWING JESUS. WALK WITH HIM EVERY DAY AND DISCOVER THE WONDERFUL LIFE HE HAS IN STORE FOR YOU!

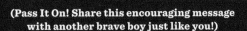

(Pass It On! Share this encouraging message with another brave boy just like you!)

WHAT'S THAT IRRITATING SOUND?

It's easy to grumble when you're asked to do something you don't want to do. You want a rewards program that lets you get by without doing a chore, or maybe there's someone else in the family who could do it this time.

Requests for help come at the worst times. You have a friend over, you're playing a game, or you're tired. You wish the whole *chore* thing could be planned without your participation.

Sometimes whining sounds like gibberish to your family. They may not understand what you're saying, but they know it's irritating.

God's Word says something like, "Quit complaining, whining, and whimpering. That's what people who don't know God do. You're supposed help people see Jesus, not irritate them with the sound of your pity parties."

When you think about what God does for you, any complaining seems disrespectful. Try thanking God. It changes the sound of complaints to words of praise.

Do all things without grumbling or disputing,
that you may be blameless and innocent, children of
God without blemish in the midst of a crooked and
twisted generation, among whom you shine as lights
in the world, holding fast to the word of life.
PHILIPPIANS 2:14–16 ESV

WHEN YOU CHANGE YOUR COMPLAINTS TO WORDS OF PRAISE, OTHERS WILL TAKE NOTICE. YOU'LL BE HELPING PEOPLE SEE JESUS!

(Pass It On! Share this encouraging message with another brave boy just like you!)

POWER OF GOD

Every couple of months, a local youth group serves lunch at a soup kitchen. As they help hand out the food, they see a side of life they wouldn't normally see. Men, women, and even kids come to the shelter for a meal. They have so little. . .when the kids from the youth group have so much.

Why do some people live better than others? Why can't God, with all His power, come in and change things. . .make things fair? The Bible says that the Jews demanded signs. They wanted God to show His power in a big way. They wanted Him to blow their minds, do something flashy.

Isn't that what we want? For God to do something flashy and take care of whatever problem we see in our lives or in other people's lives? While we may not understand God's ways, He is always at work. His wisdom is much greater than any solution our minds can create.

Where is the man who thinks he knows a lot?
Where is the man who thinks he has all the
answers? God has made the wisdom of this
world look foolish. In His wisdom, He did not
allow man to come to know Him through the
wisdom of this world. It pleased God to save
men from the punishment of their sins
through preaching the Good News.
1 Corinthians 1:20–21 NLV

Open your eyes to the power
of God at work around you.
His wisdom and love are
so much greater than
anything we could
possibly imagine.

NOTHING LEFT TO LEARN?

When you're filled with pride, you believe everyone already knows how cool you are; but if they don't, then you're ready to pass out posters listing all the reasons why you're better than just about anyone in your zip code. You walk and talk a certain way, and then try to make people think they should be honored you decided to notice them.

This may seem like a good way to prove you're awesome, but most other people don't see the same thing. They're paying a lot of attention to your actions, which seem to say, "You will never be as important as me."

Instead of people liking you more, they end up not wanting to be around you. Pride gets about the same reaction as someone showing up to a fancy restaurant in a clown suit. You get noticed, but not in a good way.

God's Word says there is more hope for a fool than for someone full of pride. Maybe that's because the fool can learn while the prideful person never believes they have anything left to learn.

There is more hope for fools than
for people who think they are wise.
PROVERBS 26:12 NLT

PRIDE DOESN'T LOOK GOOD ON ANYONE! WHEN YOU PUSH ASIDE YOUR PRIDE, IT MAKES ROOM FOR OTHERS AND HONORS GOD!

(Pass It On! Share this encouraging message with another brave boy just like you!)

GREAT EXPECTATIONS

We all have expectations. Sometimes what we expect doesn't match up with what really is. When that happens, we feel confused or frustrated or even let down.

When Jesus walked the earth, the Jews were looking for a Messiah. They were expecting a certain type of savior. . .one who would free them from their Roman captivity. What they got was Jesus. He wasn't at all what they expected! He didn't come to start a military revolution. He came with a different agenda altogether.

Why is Jesus different? He is *the* Messiah and the Son of God. He came to give us life in His name. The book of John was written to give you evidence so that you would believe the truth about Jesus. He offers something greater than freedom from earthly troubles. He is the path to eternal life. He far exceeds our expectations!

Jesus said to him, "Thomas, because you have seen Me, you believe. Those are happy who have never seen Me and yet believe!" Jesus did many other powerful works in front of His followers. They are not written in this book. But these are written so you may believe that Jesus is the Christ, the Son of God. When you put your trust in Him, you will have life that lasts forever through His name.
JOHN 20:29–31 NLV

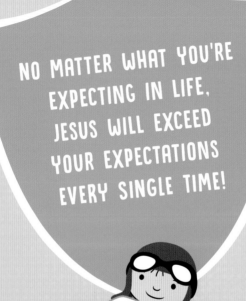

NO MATTER WHAT YOU'RE EXPECTING IN LIFE, JESUS WILL EXCEED YOUR EXPECTATIONS EVERY SINGLE TIME!

(Pass It On! Share this encouraging message with another brave boy just like you!)

LIVE IN PEACE

When we don't get along with others, it's usually because we don't agree. The other person may not like your ideas, or you may not like theirs. When people disagree, they usually get angry. Some people will hurt others when they're angry. Some will hurt back. Some never forgive.

We don't have to agree with others to live in peace with them. When we hurt someone because they hurt us, we can expect the hurt to continue.

If arguing isn't bad enough, there are many sins that follow. You could wind up stealing something that doesn't belong to you or wanting something that can never be yours, and fighting can even lead to murder.

Standing up for what's right is a good thing. Fighting in order to have something that isn't yours is not.

What is causing the quarrels and fights among you? Don't they come from the evil desires at war within you? You want what you don't have, so you scheme and kill to get it. You are jealous of what others have, but you can't get it, so you fight and wage war to take it away from them.

JAMES 4:1–2 NLT

REMEMBER THIS: ARGUMENTS RARELY LEAD TO HAPPY ENDINGS, AND THEY'RE NOT A GOOD USE OF YOUR TIME.

(Pass It On! Share this encouraging message with another brave boy just like you!)

THE WISE REMEMBER

Sometimes all we can think of is ourselves. We remember the things someone did to us, the homework we don't think we have time to do, and a family member we think is rude. We think only about our problems and accomplishments, but when it's all about us there's no room for God.

God's Word says we're wise when we think about the ways God shows us His love. We find it in the way He created the sun to shine and the moon to glow. He loves us in providing food to eat. His love is found in the air we breathe, the things we enjoy, the forgiveness He offers, and how He rescued us from the punishment of sin.

Look hard enough and find God's love in the affection of a pet, the company of friends, and in people who make you smile.

God has blessed you. Spend time remembering what He has done for you and watch your attitude change from thinking about *you* to thinking about God and the *other* people He made.

Let the one who is wise heed these things and
ponder the loving deeds of the Lord.
PSALM 107:43 NIV

FOCUS YOUR THOUGHTS ON GOD AND HIS FAITHFULNESS TO YOU. WHEN YOU DO THAT, YOU'LL BECOME WISE.

(Pass It On! Share this encouraging message with another brave boy just like you!)

INVEST WISELY

When you take money to the bank and put it in a savings account, it will earn more money. This is called an investment. Wise people invest in decisions that lead to God-honoring futures.

God wants us to invest our time, money, and choices wisely. Since our future is with Him in heaven, it doesn't make a lot of sense to try to look, act, and sound like everyone around us.

Spending a lot of time doing things that don't help us become more like Jesus teaches us to be more like people who don't know Him.

We should prepare to live in heaven. This means we change the way we think, we learn God's plans to make us more like Him, and we follow those plans.

When people can't tell a difference between us and someone who doesn't follow Jesus, then we might need to ask God for some help. He's always ready to lead when we're ready to follow.

Don't copy the behavior and customs of this world,
but let God transform you into a new person
by changing the way you think. Then you
will learn to know God's will for you,
which is good and pleasing and perfect.
ROMANS 12:2 NLT

MAKE EVERY MINUTE OF YOUR LIFE COUNT. SEEK GOD'S WORD TO DISCOVER HOW HE WANTS YOU TO INVEST YOUR LIFE.

(Pass It On! Share this encouraging message with another brave boy just like you!)

KINGDOM CURIOSITY

Are you curious? Some people like to know how things work while others are curious about history, sports, or music.

We should be curious, but God wants us to be most curious about the future He has planned for us.

We can be curious about many things that will never lead us closer to God. These distractions may be a waste of time and delay our learning what God wants us to do.

God's Word never says, "Seek first gaming cheat codes," or "Seek first the football field," or even, "Seek first to get straight As." While there may be nothing wrong with gaming, sports, or schoolwork, God tells us to "seek the Kingdom of God."

Many people know they should seek God, but never really do. A church service on the weekend is about as curious as they get. God wants us to be even more inquisitive. He gives us permission to be curious every day of the year.

Get curious.

"Seek the Kingdom of God above all else, and live righteously, and he will give you everything you need."
MATTHEW 6:33 NLT

Be curious. Dig into God's Word.
It will help you to understand
the best way to live,
the reasons to love,
and the amazing gifts
He has for you!

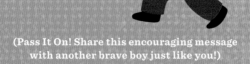

THE WORDS WE SPEAK

Words are pretty important. But it's not just the words; it's also *how* we say them. You can speak the right words, but in a way that causes others to think you don't really mean them.

Sometimes you can use words that distract people from what you're really saying. This can be confusing to the person who hears you speak.

We may tell other people that we love God and want to follow Him, but then use what God calls "foul or abusive language." These may be words we hear other people say every day, but when we say them we make people think we aren't serious about following God. Why? These words don't show what God is like. God wants us to speak differently.

It's easy to be abusive in the way we talk or use language we know is inappropriate, but God says, "Let everything you say be good and helpful, so that your words will be an encouragement to those who hear them."

Don't use foul or abusive language. Let everything you say be good and helpful, so that your words will be an encouragement to those who hear them.
EPHESIANS 4:29 NLT

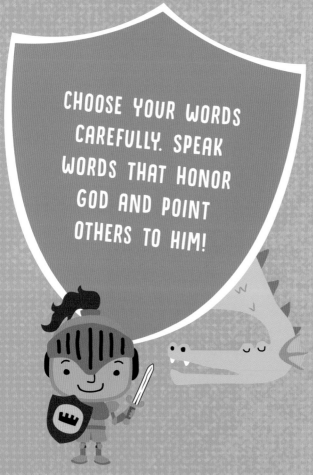

CHOOSE YOUR WORDS CAREFULLY. SPEAK WORDS THAT HONOR GOD AND POINT OTHERS TO HIM!

(Pass It On! Share this encouraging message with another brave boy just like you!)

START WELL—FINISH STRONG

>>>———————————→

The Bible has stories of people who blew it. God rescued murderers, liars, cheaters, and all sorts of untrustworthy people. Maybe He wanted to share their stories so we would see that He really can change the way we think, act, and live.

We see so many people who may have started badly, but they end up finishing well. God loves to rescue people from sinful choices.

But God is also interested in helping us learn to make good choices and to make those a part of our everyday lives. We aren't perfect, but we can make following God a priority. God wants us to start well and finish strong.

Daniel was one of those individuals. He trusted God, obeyed His laws, and served in difficult conditions.

If you've heard of Daniel, you may remember that he was thrown in a pit filled with hungry lions as a punishment for praying. He trusted God and was kept safe.

> [Daniel said], "Praise be to the name of God
> for ever and ever; wisdom and power are
> his. . . . He gives wisdom to the wise and
> knowledge to the discerning."
> DANIEL 2:20–21 NIV

NO MATTER WHERE YOU ARE, GOD IS THERE WITH A RESCUE PLAN! IF YOU ASK HIM, HE WILL RESCUE YOU FROM BAD CHOICES.

(Pass It On! Share this encouraging message with another brave boy just like you!)

ENCOURAGEMENT IN THE STORIES

Why should we read God's Word? Let's look at the verse below.

The first reason is "to teach us." We learn when we read the Bible. It's an instruction manual, textbook, biography, and songbook; and it includes poetry. We can learn about God through what we read.

The second reason is that we get to see the result of what happens when people live through difficult experiences while they follow God. We might think it's not worth following when we're having bad days, but if we read the Bible we find all kinds of people who discovered that God has always been willing and able to take care of them.

Another reason for spending time with God is finding encouragement in the stories. We all need to be encouraged. You might face a situation that you're sure no one has ever faced. The Bible can prove you've never been alone.

You'll also find hope when you grow closer to God. Stand strong. God will help you through the most difficult days.

Everything that was written in the past was written to teach us, so that through the endurance taught in the Scriptures and the encouragement they provide we might have hope.

ROMANS 15:4 NIV

Set aside time to spend with God each day. Learn more about Him in His Word, the Bible. You'll see that He is a hope-giver and encourager and He'll help you through anything!

HE NEVER DISAPPOINTS

Your friend promised to hang out with you after school. He never showed up, and he never called. You were excited about a trip at school, but at the last minute it was canceled. You had been waiting to see a movie for a long time, but when you arrived at the theater it was no longer showing.

Disappointment. It's like a lost kitten that keeps following us when we wish it would go home and leave us alone. Our plans are interrupted by disappointment. We struggle to hope when we're disappointed. Trusting others is more difficult when disappointment shows up.

God's Word says, "Those who hope in me will not be disappointed." More than anyone you know, God can be trusted. When He says He will do something, it's more than a promise, it's a guarantee. He accepts, forgives, loves, provides, brings peace, offers grace, saves, and rewards those who make seeking Him their number one priority.

Whenever you find yourself disappointed, remember that if God really is the most important priority in your life, then the most important part of your life will never disappoint. Hope in Him.

[God said] "Those who hope in
me will not be disappointed."
ISAIAH 49:23 NIV

GOD'S WORD CAN BE TRUSTED. IT'S GUARANTEED. WHEN GOD MAKES A PROMISE, HE ALWAYS KEEPS IT!

(Pass It On! Share this encouraging message with another brave boy just like you!)

GOD IS FOR US

➤————————➤

Some days everything goes wrong. You forget your school project, wake up late, and your dog visits the trash can buffet in the kitchen.

When you get to school, you can't find your best friend, you studied the wrong pages for a test, and they're playing a game you hate in gym class.

We can be discouraged for many reasons, but when we pay attention to God's Word we discover there isn't any real reason to be frustrated. God is for us.

Think about that for a minute. All the mean things in the world can't stop God from being for us. Nothing anyone can do will stop God from helping us, teaching us, and loving us.

Everyone around us can work overtime to discourage us, but God wrote His words to encourage us. He wants us to be successful, confident, and wise. While He knows we will be discouraged from time to time, He wants that discouragement to end the moment we remember some really great news. *God is for us.*

If God is for us, who can ever be against us?
Romans 8:31 nlt

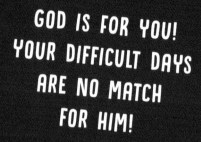

GOD IS FOR YOU!
YOUR DIFFICULT DAYS
ARE NO MATCH
FOR HIM!

(Pass It On! Share this encouraging message
with another brave boy just like you!)

CHOOSE HONESTY

→

People have lots of reasons for lying. Maybe they think a lie will get them out of trouble or will save them from getting into trouble. It doesn't matter why a person decides to lie; God tells us to *stop lying*.

Lying is part of our old self. When we follow God, we learn the value of telling the truth, and honesty makes a positive difference in how people think of us.

Accepting God's rescue plan means we're new and different. We help others, share Jesus, and become more like what God wants us to be.

When we lie, we have to remember each story we tell; but when we tell different stories to different people, it's very hard to keep every story straight. Getting caught in a lie makes it harder for other people to trust us.

Make things easier and tell the truth.

Do not lie to each other, since you have taken off your old self with its practices and have put on the new self, which is being renewed in knowledge in the image of its Creator.
Colossians 3:9–10 NIV

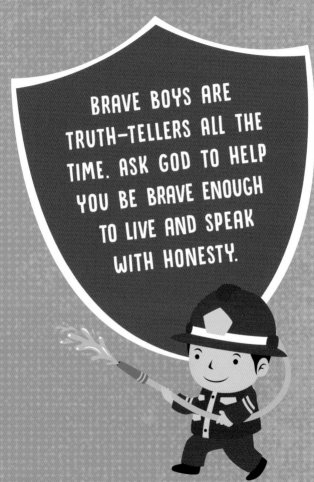

BRAVE BOYS ARE TRUTH-TELLERS ALL THE TIME. ASK GOD TO HELP YOU BE BRAVE ENOUGH TO LIVE AND SPEAK WITH HONESTY.

(Pass It On! Share this encouraging message with another brave boy just like you!)

DISTRACTIONS

Maybe you've said something like, "God, today I'm going to read Your words, and I'm going to see if I can figure out what they mean." You really want to, but your mind gets distracted, and you can't seem to think clearly.

You remember something you did last week, something you want to do tonight, a favorite television show, or a sports team. Your mind can think of almost anything but what you want it to think about. Talk about frustrating.

Distractions are normal. They happen to the best of us. Maybe that's why spending time with God is so important. It helps us learn to think about what He wants us to do. When you make meeting with God as normal as eating lunch, you may be surprised at how much you can learn between the distractions.

They may never completely go away, but distractions should never stop you from joining God on the adventure of your life.

*I will study your commandments
and reflect on your ways.*
PSALM 119:15 NLT

WHAT ARE THE THINGS THAT DISTRACT YOU FROM SPENDING TIME WITH GOD? ASK HIM TO HELP YOU BE WISE AND CHOOSE THE BEST WAY— HIS WAY.

(Pass It On! Share this encouraging message
with another brave boy just like you!)

EVERYONE'S INVITED

In the beginning, God created everything and called it "good." The things we see. The things we don't see. The things on earth and in heaven. God made it all.

Nothing can exist without God. He's the only one who can hold everything together.

God's Word says the only one who is truly good is God, but because God created all of us, not one of us is better than another. God doesn't look at our skin color or address. God always looks at our hearts. People with all kinds of skin colors can make good decisions. People with all kinds of skin colors can make bad decisions.

Our choices, not our culture or background, tell the most about who we are. The best news is we're *all* invited to follow God.

For in him all things were created: things in heaven and on earth, visible and invisible, whether thrones or powers or rulers or authorities; all things have been created through him and for him. He is before all things, and in him all things hold together.
COLOSSIANS 1:16–17 NIV

REMEMBER THIS:
ALL PEOPLE CAN LOVE
GOD, AND GOD LOVES
ALL PEOPLE!

(Pass It On! Share this encouraging message
with another brave boy just like you!)

CURIOUS ENOUGH TO KEEP ASKING

Why did God give us the Bible? He knew we would have questions. God isn't upset when we ask questions, but He wants us to trust Him—even if we don't like the answer.

Many people ask questions about why God does what He does, but they don't really want an answer. Their questions can show that they don't trust God or that they are trying to make others doubt Him.

God's answers always help make our faith stronger.

It's easy to doubt when you've never seen something with your own eyes. This is why faith is important. Faith is being able to believe something is true and trustworthy without seeing it first.

Ask questions and then open the Bible. That's where you'll find answers. When you don't read God's Word, it can be easy to be confused.

When we have doubts, faith steps in and believes God can make us wise enough to understand, patient enough to wait, and curious enough to keep asking.

If you need wisdom, ask our generous God,
and he will give it to you. He will not rebuke
you for asking. But when you ask him,
be sure that your faith is in God alone.
JAMES 1:5–6 NLT

HAVE A QUESTION FOR GOD? ASK HIM AND THEN READ HIS WORD. HIS ANSWERS ARE ALWAYS PERFECT!

A SERVANT'S HEART

The Bible talks about the hungry, the thirsty, the stranger, the person in need of clothes, the sick, and the prisoner. There have been a lot of good ministries started just for these people. Many churches support these ministries with money. Other churches send volunteers. But how often do we really see the hurting and helpless around us?

Standing up for a classmate who is being bullied, sitting with a new student at lunch, helping your little sister after she falls off her bike—these are all ways of offering God's love to those around us. Having a servant's heart means noticing "the least of these" and acting on it.

"Then those that are right with God will say, 'Lord, when did we see You hungry and feed You? When did we see You thirsty and give You a drink? When did we see You a stranger and give You a room? When did we see You had no clothes and we gave You clothes? And when did we see You sick or in prison and we came to You?' Then the King will say, 'For sure, I tell you, because you did it to one of the least of My brothers, you have done it to Me.'"
MATTHEW 25:37–40 NLV

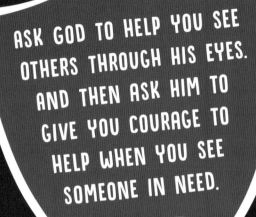

ASK GOD TO HELP YOU SEE OTHERS THROUGH HIS EYES. AND THEN ASK HIM TO GIVE YOU COURAGE TO HELP WHEN YOU SEE SOMEONE IN NEED.

(Pass It On! Share this encouraging message
with another brave boy just like you!)

THEY PLAY ON OUR TEAM

You go to church with people you know. You sing with them every weekend and go to school with some of them during the week. You can feel really comfortable at your church, and that's a good thing.

Now think about what it would be like to bring Christians from every nation you can think of and put them in the same building for a weekend church service. How comfortable would you feel?

Sometimes we may think the only Christians we can trust and talk to are those who go to our church or school. We're comfortable with the people who live on our block or play on our team.

Our verse is saying something like, "There isn't eagle, bear, buffalo, or ram. There isn't Asian, Caucasian, African American, or Spanish. We work for one team—God's."

Sometimes we don't act like it, but those are the rules according to God's playbook. He never wants divisions between people. He gave us a plan to be united. That should happen when anyone accepts God's rescue plan of salvation.

There is neither Jew nor Gentile,
neither slave nor free, nor is there male and
female, for you are all one in Christ Jesus.
GALATIANS 3:28 NIV

Think of all the people in this big wide world who love Jesus. How many of them have you never met? Ask God to help you love those people too!

EASIER TO BLAME

We all sin. God told us we would. Sometimes we don't want to admit it.

It's easier to blame others. Maybe you want to blame a family member who made you mad or a teacher who gave more homework than you thought was fair.

When the first man and woman (Adam and Eve) committed the first sin, they didn't search for God and apologize. They didn't ask for forgiveness. They didn't even admit what they'd done. Adam blamed Eve for giving him a piece of fruit from the forbidden tree, and Eve blamed the serpent for being deceitful. Men, women, boys, and girls have been blaming one another ever since.

All of us can come up with an excuse for our sin. God never accepts excuses, but He does offer forgiveness when we admit we're wrong.

It's hard to be friends with God when we refuse to be honest with Him. Sometimes we forget He already knows what we do. Trying to hide or blaming others never works.

Then the LORD God asked the woman,
"What have you done?" "The serpent deceived
me," she replied. "That's why I ate it."
GENESIS 3:13 NLT

BE 100 PERCENT HONEST WITH GOD. TALK TO HIM AND TELL HIM YOU'RE SORRY. HE'LL FORGIVE YOU RIGHT AWAY!

(Pass It On! Share this encouraging message with another brave boy just like you!)

TRADING FAILURE FOR SUCCESS

God knows everything. We know only what we learn. Sometimes we learn through mistakes.

Sin is always failure, but failure isn't always sin. Doing something God tells us not to do is sin. Trying something that just doesn't work out is failure. But we don't have to learn everything through trial and error because God already gave us His commands, so we don't really have an excuse for not learning them.

God knows we will fail, so He shows His power through forgiveness of our sins and encouragement in our failures.

The things we can't do on our own are things that God has no trouble doing. When we're weak, we shouldn't be surprised to see how God's strength can accomplish what we can't.

As Christians, we're part of God's family. As part of God's family, we can talk to God about anything. He wants to teach us through our failures and to help us in our weakness. He loves turning failure into success.

[Jesus said], "My grace is all you need. My power works best in weakness." So now I am glad to boast about my weaknesses, so that the power of Christ can work through me.

2 CORINTHIANS 12:9 NLT

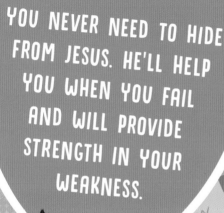

YOU NEVER NEED TO HIDE FROM JESUS. HE'LL HELP YOU WHEN YOU FAIL AND WILL PROVIDE STRENGTH IN YOUR WEAKNESS.

(Pass It On! Share this encouraging message with another brave boy just like you!)

MUSIC

Since the dawn of time, humans have had a connection with music. It's a deeply personal form of communication that reaches to our very core.

Regardless of the type of music that draws you, you should take an honest look at it. The Bible says, "Each tree is recognized by its own fruit." If music is the tree, then the words are the fruit. What are the words communicating? Are they consistent with what is found in the Bible? When you listen to music, you are storing up things in your heart. . .either good or evil. There is no right or wrong kind of music. All genres of music have good and bad songs. . .even praise music! It's up to you to decide if they line up with what the Bible teaches. That takes effort on your part. It's an important challenge because the Bible says, "For the mouth speaks what the heart is full of."

"Each tree is recognized by its own fruit.
People do not pick figs from thornbushes, or grapes
from briers. A good man brings good things out of
the good stored up in his heart, and an evil
man brings evil things out of the evil stored
up in his heart. For the mouth speaks
what the heart is full of."
LUKE 6:44–46 NIV

What kind of music is on your playlist? Hint: If it Doesn't honor God, ask Him for the courage to make the necessary changes.

(Pass It On! Share this encouraging message with another brave boy just like you!)

GETTING READY FOR
THE NEXT PHASE

God is looking for faithful guys your age. His plan for their future is amazing, but He knows they'll need training for the next phase of their adventure.

Imagine if God were to say to you, "I have something only you can do, and I want you to start training today so you'll be ready."

You'd probably get excited. "What do You want me to do, God?" you ask.

"Obey your parents and clean your room" is the reply.

Wait! What does that story have to do with God's plan? God often asks us to do simple, but less exciting things to see if we'll be faithful in doing our best. We learn patience, obedience, and faithfulness when we do small things well.

If we can be trusted with small things, we can be trusted with bigger things. If we can't be trusted to take care of the small things, God might need to wait until we are trustworthy to show us the next step in His training plans for us.

> [Jesus said] "Whoever can be trusted with
> very little can also be trusted with much,
> and whoever is dishonest with very little
> will also be dishonest with much."
> LUKE 16:10 NIV

GOD is looking for Brave Boys just like YOU! Ask Him What you should Be Doing to Prepare for His Wonderful Plan... and then Do it!

PERFECTLY DESIGNED

Joints allow fingers and toes to move. Your eyes let you see colors, textures, and the faces of people you know. Your ears allow you to hear music, voices, and nature.

Our bodies are the result of a loving God who knew we would need fingers that bend in order to hold a cup of water, brains that understand color, and ears inspired by sound.

God crafted you into a marvelous creation that is extremely complex and perfectly designed.

The psalm writer shows us that thanking God is a great way to respond when we think about the way God made us, even when we don't think we're perfect because we see something about ourselves we don't like, or when accident, injury, or disease makes us feel less than perfect. Our bodies aren't forever, but our souls can live with God for eternity. As amazing as our bodies are, God is more interested in the condition of our souls. When we thank God for the creation of our bodies, it indicates our souls are in pretty good shape.

Thank you for making me so
wonderfully complex! Your workmanship
is marvelous—how well I know it.
PSALM 139:14 NLT

YOU ARE ONE-OF-A-KIND. . .
CRAFTED BY ALMIGHTY
GOD! THANK HIM TODAY
FOR THE AMAZING
MASTERPIECE THAT
IS YOU!

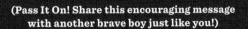

(Pass It On! Share this encouraging message
with another brave boy just like you!)

THE RIGHT NEXT STEPS

You might have a career in the back of your mind that you're planning to go into when you finish school. You might be thinking of college, a trade school, or a whole lot of training.

It's possible all you're really thinking about is what you'll have at your next meal, if you can beat your high score on a game you like, or how late you'll get to stay up when you're older.

We all have plans, and we're pretty certain we can make them happen, but the simple act of living can change our plans. We can adjust and adapt to the best of our ability, but even that may not be enough.

Our best decision will be to let God change our plans if He wants.

God knows everything about you. He knows your future and doesn't want you to struggle to figure it out. If we can accept that God's plan is much better than ours, it will be easier to let Him help us take the right next steps.

We can make our plans,
but the Lord determines our steps.
PROVERBS 16:9 NLT

HOLD your plans loosely and allow GOD to adjust them as He knows Best. He will never steer you in the wrong direction.

(Pass It On! Share this encouraging message with another brave boy just like you!)

JOY INSPIRED

>>>————————>

Adults buy investments because they want to earn more than they spend. They save in order to keep more than they had. They're careful about what they buy because they don't want to be wasteful.

God's Word says that generous people prosper; but how can you prosper when you give away something without expecting anything in return?

Giving to others builds relationships. When you help others, there's a good chance they won't forget your kindness. Instead of money being your focus, invest in friendships that will last long after the money is gone.

There's no price on the value of people who care about you. You can't buy it, beg for it, or think you'll always have it.

The generous prosper because they understand money doesn't deliver joy, but joy can be recognized in a generous heart. We give because we've received. We share because someone shared with us. We love because God loved us.

Generous people stand out to those who are used to seeing selfishness. They are remembered. They are given gratitude. They rarely regret their own generosity.

The generous will prosper; those who refresh others will themselves be refreshed.
PROVERBS 11:25 NLT

Always Be generous
With your time, talents,
and treasures—you'll
never regret it!
Generosity is an
investment that
Pays Dividends
in joy!

(Pass It On! Share this encouraging message
with another brave boy just like you!)

BULLIES

Bullies come in all shapes and sizes. The Bible's most famous bully is Goliath, a nine-foot-nine-inch tall Philistine. Each day, he taunted the Israelites to send their best warrior to fight him. Whoever was left standing would win the war. The Israelites were shaking in their boots! No one wanted to fight him. Then David, who was too young to be a soldier, showed up with food for his older brothers. David knew that it was God who had been insulted, not man. So it would be God standing up against the bully through David. . .and God is much bigger than Goliath!

You don't always have to get in the middle of a fight to fight a bully. Like David, realize that God is bigger than any bully. Befriend those who are picked on. Kindness can go a long way.

Saul said to David, "You are not able to go and fight against this Philistine. You are only a young man, while he has been a man of war since he was young." But David said to Saul. . ."The Lord Who saved me from the foot of the lion and from the foot of the bear, will save me from the hand of this Philistine."
1 SAMUEL 17:33–34, 37 NLV

GOD IS ON YOUR SIDE TODAY AND ALWAYS. IN THE PRESENCE OF A BULLY, ASK HIM FOR THE COURAGE TO STAND UP FOR WHAT'S RIGHT.

(Pass It On! Share this encouraging message with another brave boy just like you!)

CONTROLLED STRENGTH

Maybe you've been told to act like a gentleman. Perhaps you thought that meant to act like a man who is weak, so you stayed quiet and didn't talk to anyone.

When you understand what being a gentleman really is, you might have a different opinion about what you're supposed to do in order to show this quality to others.

Being a gentleman doesn't mean to intentionally show weakness. When you're asked to be a gentleman, you should remember that God gave you many great strengths. There are things you're really good at. Being a guy is an active, adventurous job; but being a gentleman doesn't mean you try to deny all the things that make you who you are. The best description of being a gentleman is *controlled strength*.

Think about a car. It has an accelerator that makes the car move. Like that car, a gentleman moves carefully so he doesn't overpower conversations, games, or situations. He remains strong, but in control. No matter the occasion, it's always a good decision to be a gentleman.

Let's not merely say that we love each other;
let us show the truth by our actions.
1 JOHN 3:18 NLT

Are you in control of your strengths? Ask God to help you be a gentleman who has a handle on your responses and actions.

IN SEARCH OF WISE GUYS

You want to be wise, right? You want God to help you learn things you should know, to respond to others in a way that honors God and gives proof that you're walking with the one who rescued you.

God's wisdom is pure. It's not influenced by hatred, revenge, or anger. It's a perfect model to follow.

God's wisdom is peace-loving, which means it's not interested in battle, but in demonstrating qualities of peaceful solution.

God's wisdom is considerate because it seeks to honor others.

God's wisdom is submissive and pays attention to the whole story.

God's wisdom is merciful and offers forgiveness.

God's wisdom is impartial and never makes decisions based on where you live or your cultural background.

God's wisdom is sincere and never deceitful.

You might want God's wisdom for yourself. His wisdom pays attention to what God has already said and subtracts emotions from issues, so when a decision is made it's fair because all sides have been considered.

The wisdom that comes from heaven is first of all pure; then peace-loving, considerate, submissive, full of mercy and good fruit, impartial and sincere.

JAMES 3:17 NIV

Think before you act. . .
EVERY SINGLE TIME. Brave
Boys show wisdom in
their decisions and actions.
When you demonstrate
true wisdom, others will
see proof that you're
walking with God!

(Pass It On! Share this encouraging message
with another brave boy just like you!)

SECRETS BETRAYED

→

People need to trust you when sharing something they wouldn't tell anyone else.

Imagine being sworn to secrecy. You solemnly promise silence. The secret is told, and your friend leaves believing their confidence is safe. As far as you're concerned, it *is* safe. You have no plans to tell anyone.

However, the more you think about it, the more impressive and powerful the secret becomes. You know something no one else knows. Suddenly you're considering the idea of sharing the secret. The harder you try to stop it, the more it wants to come out.

When the words finally tumble from your lips to other ears, you think the only way to minimize the damage is to swear that person to secrecy, but the cycle is set to reboot and start all over again with worse results.

The Bible tells us to stop gossiping, and then it tells us to stay away from people who gossip.

A gossip betrays another person, spreads information that may not be true, and can hurt the person who trusted them with their secret.

A gossip betrays a confidence;
so avoid anyone who talks too much.
PROVERBS 20:19 NIV

BRAVE BOYS ARE
TRUSTWORTHY FRIENDS.
FOLLOW GOD'S EXAMPLE:
BE A PROMISE-
KEEPER.

(Pass It On! Share this encouraging message
with another brave boy just like you!)

FOR THE GOD WHO HAS EVERYTHING

➤➤➤————————————➤

At the very center of gratitude is the understanding that someone is more important than we are. We can't thank someone without recognizing they did something for us that we couldn't do for ourselves, no matter how hard we tried.

In order to show gratitude to God, we need to acknowledge that He is God. We admit that He made us and takes care of us.

This is why we sing songs of praise and worship in church. We tell God in song that we're His people and we're grateful for everything He does. We see all the beautiful things He created, and it's impressive enough that we can't help but worship Him. Even His name is so honorable that we should never use it in a dishonorable way.

We have always been important to God. Maybe a good question is, "How important is God to us?"

Acknowledge that the Lord is God! He made us, and we are his. We are his people, the sheep of his pasture. Enter his gates with thanksgiving; go into his courts with praise. Give thanks to him and praise his name.
PSALM 100:3–4 NLT

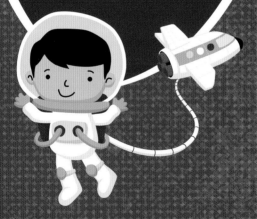

GOD gave you life. He offers rescue, forgiveness, and grace. His creation is for your enjoyment. He gives you courage, hope, and love. He's yours, and you're His!

(Pass It On! Share this encouraging message with another brave boy just like you!)

TALKING WITH GOD

Have you ever been angry with God? I mean, really *really* angry? Things in your life might not be going the way you want, and you wonder where God is!

The Bible tells us about a man named Elijah. He is a prophet of God and has just been used to perform a mighty miracle. But now the king's wife has put a hit out on his life. Elijah runs, scared, and hides. Eventually God tells him to stand on a mountain. There are powerful winds, an earthquake, and a fire, but that wasn't God. God began to speak in a gentle whisper.

Sometimes we expect God to rescue us with a big, loud, thunderous show of strength. Our talking to God becomes a list of wants or demands. It's okay to tell God how we are feeling. Elijah did. But we need to wait and listen for the gentle whisper of God.

"Go out and stand before me on the mountain,"
the Lord told him. And as Elijah stood there, the
Lord passed by, and a mighty windstorm hit the
mountain. It was such a terrible blast that the
rocks were torn loose, but the Lord was not in the
wind. After the wind there was an earthquake,
but the Lord was not in the earthquake.
And after the earthquake there was a fire,
but the Lord was not in the fire. And after the
fire there was the sound of a gentle whisper.
1 Kings 19:11–12 nlt

GOD is speaking to you—
He cares about every
big and small thing
you're going through.
Are you listening
for His voice?